To Lucy, Matthew, & Virginia

Evaluating Tree Defects

Copyright © 2001 by Ed Hayes

Published by Safetrees • 532 22nd St NE, Rochester, MN 55906 • September, 2001

E-mail: ehayes@safetrees.com

Website: www.safetrees.com

All rights reserved. No part of this publication may be reproduced in any form or by any means without prior written permission from the publisher.

ISBN: 0-9714128-0-4

How To Use This Field Guide

The purpose for this field guide is to assist the Arborist, Community Forester, and Resource Manager in evaluating tree defects.

The guidelines presented can be used to identify high-risk trees, and in some instances trees that have already failed. These guidelines are not exhaustive. Guidelines cannot be written for every situation. Evaluating tree defects is as much of an art as it is a science. Following inspections, some trees will be left behind that will fail in the next storm event. Likewise, some trees that are removed may have survived the next storm event. The guidelines allow the tree care professional to approach a highly subjective practice in an objective way.

Two methods for evaluating stem and branch decay are given. Both are based on determining the amount of sound wood in the outer wall relative to the stem/branch radius or diameter. Most experts agree that a ratio (proportion) of 30 to 35% of sound wood in the remaining wall is a threshold that requires some action be taken.

In the first method the "rules of thumb" given by Hayes are based on this ratio of sound wood to the stem/branch radius (Mattheck's 32%), and converted to inches in diameter for ease of use in the field. In the Hayes method a rule is given for increasing the sound wood requirement when cavity openings to the outside reach 20 % or more of stem circumference and again at 30%.

The second method by Bartlett is also based on this ratio, and factors in cavity openings beginning at 5% and ending at 30%. In the Bartlett method the inspector must subtract the bark thickness and use the actual stem wood diameter. It is recommended that both of these approaches be tested to determine which will best meet the needs of the tree care professional or client. Invasive techniques are performed to confirm or alleviate suspicions.

The high-risk guidelines given in this field guide pertain to trees with full crowns and targets.

The use of this ratio of sound wood to stem size is not meant to be used exclusive of a host of other contributing risk factors that must be considered.

When trees reach or fall below the threshold values or guidelines given, mitigation or removal is recommended. Mitigation can range from increasing awareness of risk to specific actions. Mitigation is possible with high risk trees depending on creative solutions involving target considerations, and reducing crown size and weight. How can the risk of failure be reduced, and the lives of valuable trees be extended? There are no clear cut guidelines for how much of the crown can be reduced to lower the risk of failure and not compromise tree health. Better answers lie ultimately in further study and trial and error.

The thresholds for root decay recommended by the Bartlett Tree Research Laboratories are presented as a starting point for Arborists to learn more about, and discuss root decay caused tree failures. Test and look for these threshold following storm events.

Learn to see the body language of trees. Recognize the subtle signs of mechanical failure and how to associate those signs with the reasons the tree is failing. When trees fail, inspect them to determine why. When a tree is removed, dissect it to determine if the right decision was made. Learn as you practice, every tree is different.

If removals are to be prioritized, a rating system is needed. See the ISA manual, (Mattheny and Clark).

Finally, all trees have the potential to fail, fortunately only a relative few actually do. Trees can have defects, most do. Trees have the ability to repair some of these defects by adaptive growth. Use this field guide to make objective evaluations and informed decisions.

Evaluating Risk of Tree Failure

The Process — *Visual inspection for defects (VTA, Visual Tree Assessment), sounding for suspect decay, and probing for decay if needed, with drill, increment borer or the IML-Resi.*

Formulating a Decision — *Involves balancing several factors including multiple defects, species characteristics, location and extent of decay, crown size, ratio, and exposure, target considerations, tree value, and owner attitudes. What level of risk is the owner willing to accept?*

(3)

Leaning Trees and Root Problems

Inadequate Root Anchoring Support or Structural Weakness.

Trees with High Risk of Failure   (For trees with full crowns and targets)

Tree with excessive (30-40°) lean, and a target.

Leaning tree with recent root lifting, soil movement, mounding, or cracks in soil surface.

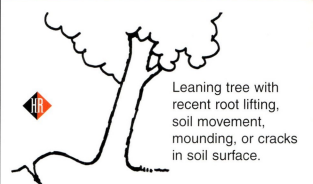

Leaning tree with horizontal cracks on the upper (tension) side and/or buckling wood or bark on the lower (compression) side.

Leaning tree with a crack through the center of the stem.

Leaning Trees and Root Problems

Leaning tree with a crack, canker, or decay on the lower stem.

(Lower risk without lean, however predisposed to storm failure)

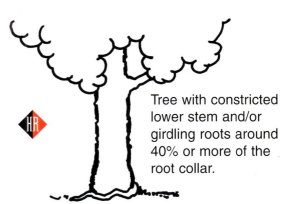

Tree with constricted lower stem and/or girdling roots around 40% or more of the root collar.

Tree with 33% or more of the roots *decayed*, or *missing*.

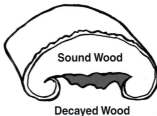

Top of Root

Sound Wood

Decayed Wood

Missing > 1/3 of major buttress roots severed within 3x(dbh).

Decayed >1/3 of major buttress roots with a sound wood thickness of < .15(dbh).

(If > 1/2 critical risk, Bartlett Tree Research, 1998).

Reduce thresholds when: decayed or missing roots are opposite a lean, on the uphill side, for low crown ratios, weak wooded species, for exposed, sensitive, or high use sites.

Evaluating Root Decay

Root decay occurs most often on old or "over mature" trees. Sites that have been disturbed by development, or by trampling as a result of high use may have above average levels of root decay.

Signs and symptoms of root collar decay.
- Loose and dead bark
- Conks, fungus fruiting structures
- Cracks in the lower trunk
- Sap flow from lower trunk
- Abnormal root flares, diminished, or loss of root flares
- Soil mounding or grade changes

If signs and symptoms of decay are present and the lower stem and roots are visible, they can be sounded with a mallet. If decay is suspected then the major buttress roots should be probed to determine the thickness of sound wood, using a drill, increment borer, or the IML-Resi according to the guidelines given above for root decay.

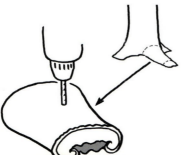

Air excavation tools can be used to examine roots below grade.

Open Cracks

Splits through the bark, extending deep into the wood.

Stem with one or more cracks, decay, or cavity (opening).

Any large branch with crack.

The stem is split in half by one or more cracks.

LOWER RISK

Stem with a single crack, seam, or rib, and no decay.

⑦
Weak Branch Unions
Multiple Stems and Poor Branch Attachments

A weak union has bark present inside the branch union.

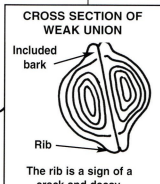

CROSS SECTION OF WEAK UNION
Included bark
Rib
The rib is a sign of a crack and decay.

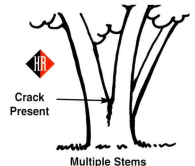

Crack Present

Multiple Stems

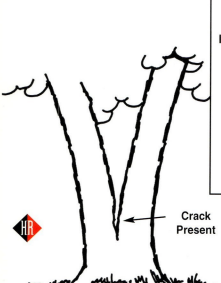

Crack Present

A weak union that is also cracked or decayed.

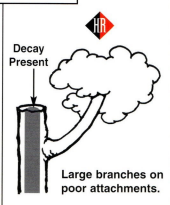

Decay Present

Large branches on poor attachments.

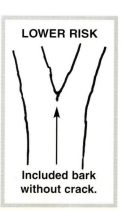

LOWER RISK

Included bark without crack.

Cankers

**Area of dead, sunken, or missing bark.
Cankers include diseases and mechanical wounds.**

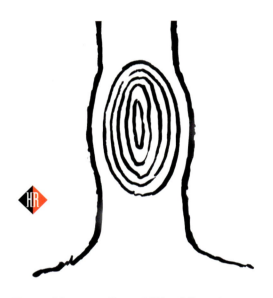

Tree with more than 40% of the stem cross-section affected by canker or decay.

The canker will eventually lead to a column of decay. Check for extent of decay. Probe through the canker face first. If decay is extensive, evaluate for decay with cavity.

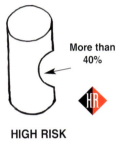

More than 40%

HIGH RISK

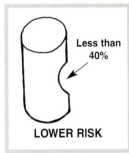

Less than 40%

LOWER RISK

Remaining cross-section should be 60% sound wood.

Cracks on Canker Face

Horizontal Cracks

Vertical Cracks

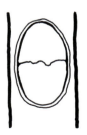

HIGH RISK

LOWER RISK

Wood Decay
Decayed Wood and Cavities

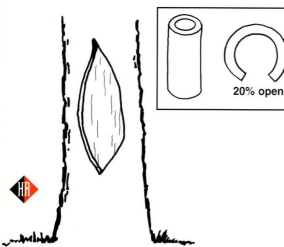

Remaining Wall Requirements

A tree needs 1 inch or more of sound wood for each 6" of stem diameter. Increase the requirement for cavities, to 1 1/2" for 20% open, and to 2" for 30% open.

20% open   30% open

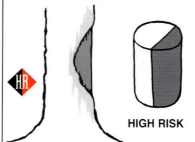

HIGH RISK

LOWER RISK

Tree with 40% or more of stem cross-section affected by decay.

Sound wood (thickness of the remaining wall) of less than 1" for each 6" of stem diameter or root collar.

Confirm weakest area by sounding. Probe for thickness of sound wood with a 1/8" drill bit, increment borer, or the IML-Resi. Average 3 or more sample depths as needed.

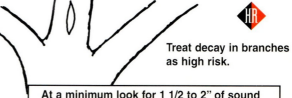

Treat decay in branches as high risk.

At a minimum look for 1 1/2 to 2" of sound wood for each 6" of branch diameter.

Evaluating Wood Decay

Additional Guidelines for Qualifying and Evaluating Wood Decay In Stems and Branches.

Method: find the average thickness of sound wood surrounding the defect by probing with a drill fitted with a 1/8" drill bit (with long flute).

- Drill into sound wood until resistance significantly decreases, indicating where decay begins.
- Extract drill bit and measure depth to decay.
- Subtract thickness of bark. Sample a minimum of 3 sites, or 1 site per 10 inches of stem/branch diameter. Increase sampling if depth to decay varies greatly.
- Calculate the average thickness of sound wood surrounding the defect. The IML-Resi or increment borer may also be used.

Corresponding to the size of the cavity opening (left column), multiply the stem/branch diameter by the percent in the center column to obtain the average minimum thickness of sound wood to support the stem/branch. **If the actual minimum thickness is less than that value, then the stem/branch represents a high risk of failure.** Critical risk: mitigation not recommended, not safe to climb.

(Bartlett Tree Research Laboratories, 1999).

D = Stem Diameter
(less 2x bark thickness)

C = Circumference = D x 3.14
(at weakest point)

W = Width of Cavity Opening

$$\text{\% Cavity Opening} = \frac{W}{C} \times 100$$

$$\text{Average Thickness of Sound Wood} = \frac{\text{Depth to Decay: Sample 1+2+3}}{\text{Number of sample sites}}$$

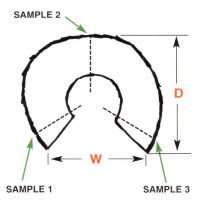

Minimum thickness of sound wood surrounding decay columns on stems and branches with and without cavity openings.

Cavity opening % of circumference	Minimum Thickness of Sound Wood Surrounding Decay	
	High Risk	**Critical Risk**
0	0.15	0.10
5%	0.17	0.11
10%	0.18	0.12
15%	0.20	0.14
20%	0.23	0.15
25%	0.26	0.17
30%	0.33	0.18

Evaluating Wood Decay (11)

Where to check for the weakest wall

Where the symptom is most pronounced.

Between root flares or within inclusions.

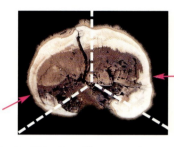

Behind the in rolling wound wood.

When to increase sound wood requirements

Increase the sound wood requirements for trees with; leaning stems/branches, unbalanced crowns, low crown ratios, multiple defects, decay in stress points, (mid-crown, bends in stems/branches, and reaction wood), asymmetrical decay column, species with weak or brittle wood characteristics, trees with decline, or on exposed, sensitive, and high use sites. *(Bartlett Tree Research Laboratories 1999).*

Asymmetrical decay

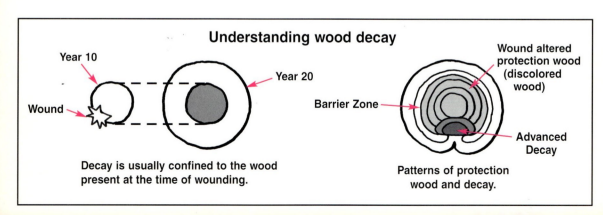

Understanding wood decay

Year 10

Wound

Year 20

Decay is usually confined to the wood present at the time of wounding.

Wound altered protection wood (discolored wood)

Barrier Zone

Advanced Decay

Patterns of protection wood and decay.

Dead Wood, Broken Hanging, or Lodged Branches

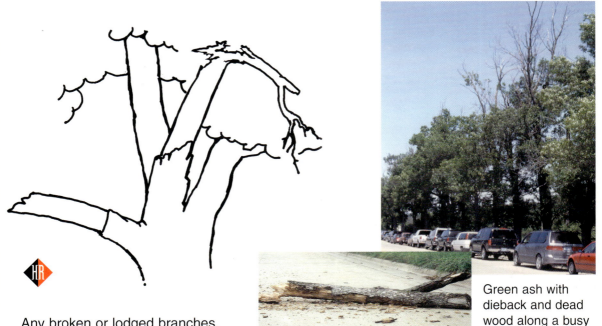

Any broken or lodged branches.
Any dead tree, top, or large branch.

Dead and decayed wood fails at different rates depending on material size, weight, and species resistance to decay.

Green ash with dieback and dead wood along a busy street.

Examples of Tree Defects

Leaning Trees and Root Problems.

Leaning white pine with shear crack through center of stem.

Buckling bark and wood on the lower compression side of this Weeping Sequoia. Remove or prop. Once a prop always a prop.

Leaning American elm with root severing below ground due to septic construction.

These elms lean naturally into the opening above a city street. Determine if the lean is natural, (phototropism-growing toward the light) or if the tree is failing. What are the signs of failure, and why?

Stem girdling roots above and below ground. Affected trees will decline and die prematurely or fail at ground line during storm events.

Cracks

Large American basswood with multiple cracks through stem and branches.

The spiral crack on this Norway maple is caused by spiral grain, a pattern in Norway maple. Spiral cracks are loaded by torsion, a lower risk of failure for trees with symmetrical crowns.

Weak Unions

Included bark inside a failed union, or compression fork.

Multiple stem Green ash with a weak union. Contact stress will push the stems apart. Cable or remove the left stem.

American elm with a poor branch attachment. High risk.

A weak union in this Valley oak failed in a storm. Nearly 70% of the cross-section remaining is sound. A good decision was made not to remove this oak. It will last for many years. Eventually decay will become a concern.

Included bark union without a crack, yet! Repair or replace.

Cankers

Canker on Bur oak with little decay. The wound is not structurally important at this time and will not be for many years.

The canker on this Bur oak occupies a larger cross-section of the stem. Behind the face a column of decay has developed. The oak must now be evaluated on the amount of sound wood in the remaining wall or cross-section.

Sugar maple with decay has a horizontal crack in the canker face. A sign of failure.

Decay

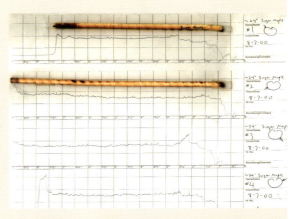

This 24" Sugar maple has 6 to 8" of sound wood in the remaining wall, as determined by the IML-Resi. Based on the rule of 1" of sound wood for each 6" of stem diameter, the requirement is 4". The ratio is 50 to 65% well above threshold. Other factors may now be evaluated to determine the tree's fate. (For computing ratio, see page 29).

For decay assessment, confirmation, and documentation by graphic output, the IML-Resi is a valuable tool. A field demonstration of the F-300-S, New York. (see: imlusa.com)

Norway spruce with decay, bulge, and a thin wall of sound wood.

Brown rots can be "undetectable", with little symptom (bulge) until very advanced.

The cavity of this 42" Silver maple (left) was filled in the late 60's when cavity filling was popular. The inrolling wound wood on each side of the opening is causing internal cracks resulting in the expanding column of decay. The cavity opening is 15%. Therefore, some additional sound wood is required based on the Bartlett method for evaluating wood decay. The ratio of the remaining wall ranges from 20% behind the inrolling wound wood to 35% on the wall opposite the cavity. Where one of the remaining walls has decreased to 20% a crack has formed (right). A sign the tree is failing.

Tropical Trees

Tropical trees are fundamentally different in two distinct ways, anatomy and energy requirements. Annual increments are indistinctive. Large amounts of food reserves (starch) are stored for flowering, reproduction, and maintenance of year round defense systems.

The Monkeypod tree is an "exceptional tree protected by city ordinance" in Honolulu. It has a dramatic, mechanically well-adapted low spreading crown. Here it creates a canopy over a busy street. It requires a large boulevard for its root system, a worthy investment.

On this Indian Banyan aerial roots are a superior mechanical adaptation for supporting enormous spreading crowns that can cover an acre or more.

Silt oak, an exotic to the Hawaiian Islands from Australia. Note the slight bulge on this 28" stem. The ratio (remaining wall, 3") is only 20%. The oak has a crack on the main stem, dieback, and has shed one large branch. Some species may be best suited to their origin, having limited use in other places around the world.

Coconut palms are high maintenance. The leaves (fronds) and coconuts must be pruned several times a year in high use areas. Adjacent to tall structures they get into trouble with phototropism. Tall thin stems increase the risk of failure.

Rainbow Eucalyptus is a large fast growing tree intolerant to improper pruning above or below ground. It has little resistance to decay.

The Tiger's Claw (Indian Coral) has shed a large branch on a calm afternoon. Branch breakage, summer branch drop, are branch failures associated with excessive end weight, large untapered branches, and weak wooded species.

Basic Tree Biomechanics

Gravity defines the weight of objects. Weight is the force the object "feels" due to gravity.

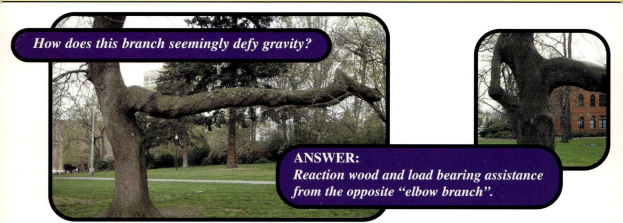

How does this branch seemingly defy gravity?

ANSWER:
Reaction wood and load bearing assistance from the opposite "elbow branch".

Strength

Strength is *determined by* the distribution and intensity of mechanical forces acting on the tree as the load changes. Strength is *dependent on* the relative amount of sound wood (cross-section) at any given point. Mechanical forces acting on the tree can change dramatically as the load changes.

◀ Before this Red pine failed in 80-mph straight-line winds the stress was highest on either side of the lower cavity opening. As the load changed dramatically to a perpendicular force the point of highest stress moved to the top of the cavity opening and increased several times in intensity. This is likely where the first crack formed at the moment the tree failed.

Basic Tree Biomechanics

Wood Strength

- Compression failures are twice (2x) as common as tension failures because wood fibers buckle under compression twice (2x) as easy as they pull apart under tension.

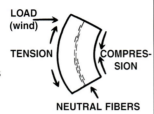

- Torsional strength (resistance to twisting) is twice (2x) as strong as bending strength.
- Dry wood is twice (2x) as strong as green wood.

Cross-section and Wood Strength

Small increases in diameter (annual increments) will add large increase in cross-sectional area and strength.

- A one-inch increase in diameter on a 20-inch tree will increase the cross sectional area by 10%, and increase the relative strength by 16%.

Stem Failures

Stem failures are greatly influenced by stem diameter (cross-section) and tree height (exposed lever arm).

- Bigger and shorter stems are stronger.
- Thinner and taller stems are weaker.
- For solitary trees a height to diameter ratio of 50 and greater is high risk. *(Mattheck, September 2001)*.
- Stem taper is a defense against stem failure.
- Doubling stem height requires almost (3x) the stem diameter to maintain taper.

- When trees from stands become edge trees, stem failures accelerate.

Wood Decay and Strength Loss

A stem with large central column of decay and thick outer remaining walls may be only slightly weaker than a solid stem.

- A central column of decay that occupies 50% of the stem cross-section is only 6% weaker than a solid stem.

(However, as larger columns of decay occupy larger cross-sections, strength loss accelerates).

- A central column of decay that occupies 70% of the stem cross-section is equivalent to the threshold of 30 to 35% ratio of sound wood to the stem/branch radius or diameter and is high risk.

(It's a fine line. Above or below this threshold, strength increases or decreases quickly and dramatically).

- As ratios decrease to 25%, stem failures accelerate.
- Exercise caution while basing assessments on ratio alone. Some western US conifers can have ratios as high as 50% with advance root decay.
- When cavity openings to the outside become large relative to the stem circumference, the sound wood requirement must be increased.
  See the guidelines by Hayes and Bartlett on pages 9 and 10.
- Asymmetrical columns of decay or off centered cavities impact stem strength only when they are relatively large and when the adjacent outer remaining wall of sound wood is thin.

Basic Tree Biomechanics

Adaptive Growth

▶ More wood is added to overloaded areas. (red arrows) Less wood is added to under loaded areas. (green arrow) There is a thin outer wall of sound wood surrounding the central column of decay, behind the the cavity opening on this Bur oak. The oak later failed during a storm and fell into the house.

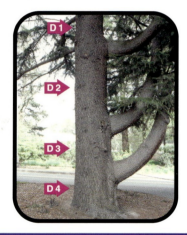

◀ There are many examples of adaptive growth. The successively larger diameters on this western spruce, D1, D2, D3, and D4, are carrying the added weight of the attached branches. Again, more wood is added to over-loaded areas.

Contact Stress

▶ Uniform stress distribution is the equilibrium of internal and external loads. As the foreign object is encountered the load bearing must be shared. Increasing the contact area with the foreign object reduces the contact stress. The foreign object now plays a role in structural support, although minor with this red oak in New Hampshire.

Basic Tree Biomechanics

Reaction Wood

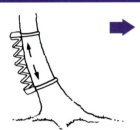

▶ **Conifers** (gymnosperms) push themselves up on the lower side with compression wood. This creates the saber spruce in Colorado.

◀ The activity is visible on the underside of this conifer branch.

▶ **Hardwoods** (angiosperms), pull themselves up on the upper side with tension wood. Reaction wood is not easy to see in hardwoods. The tension wood is visible on the upper side of this leaning American basswood. Reaction wood is most active where the localized stress is the highest.

Library, Nova Scotia Community College

Basic Tree Biomechanics

Big Trees

One of the world's largest Sitka spruce. James Causton, The Pacific Northwest.

Bigleaf maple, Rob Williams, Puget Sound, Washington

▶ Why does it appear that some big trees defy guidelines and predictions? Load, exposure, and any number of other factors all play a role in ultimate survival or failure. Big trees are more effective at building strength. Cross-section and relative strength increase quickly with additional increments on big trees. Big trees need only small increments to continue holding incredible mechanical loads. For big trees, changes in "hollowness", advance more slowly than in smaller diameter trees. It's possible that in some years there is a "net" gain in relative strength. Additionally, self-optimization into a cone shape is an asset for distributing large loads. They will survive until the precise moment of overload.

◀ *Extraordinary measures are possible for preserving one of nature's dramatic architectural designs.*

Decay Resistance of Eastern Hardwoods and Conifers

Very Resistant

Black Locust
Osage-orange
Red Mulberry

Resistant

Black walnut
Bur oak
Cedars
Chestnut
Junipers
Other White oaks
Sassafras

Moderately Resistant

Ashes
Elms
Honeylocust
Larch
Pines
Tamarack

Slightly Resistant

Black Cherry
Buckeye
Hickories
Red and Black Oaks
Sweetgum

Non-Resistant

Aspen & Poplars
Basswood
Beech
Birches
Butternut
Catalpa
Cottonwood
Fir
Hackberry
Hemlocks
Horse Chestnut
Linden
Magnolia
Maples
Paulownia
Redwood
Spruces
Sycamore
Tree of Heaven
Tulip tree
Willows
Yellow-poplar

Common Defects of Eastern Hardwoods

HARDWOODS

Species	Common Defects	Comments & Causes
Ashes	Weak unions, Decay, Cankers, Branch breakage	Weak unions are common when there is opposite bud set. Branch breakage: risk increases in trees greater than 16"dbh.
Aspens	Cankers, Decay, Stem breakage	Several canker diseases. Canker rot, disease.
Basswood	Decay, Branch breakage	Fast decay. Inrolling wound wood. Over mature and declining trees develop harp branches. Branch breakage: risk increases in trees greater than 16"dbh.
Birch	Dead wood, Decay, Root problems	Dieback; trees are easily stressed, canker rot.
Black Cherry	Dead wood, Decay, Branch breakage	A pioneer species, first in, first out. Branch breakage: risk increases in trees greater than 16"dbh.
Black Walnut	Dead wood	Generally free of defects.
Boxelder	Decay, Branch breakage	High incidence of branch failures during storm events. Little resistance to decay. Branch breakage: risk increases in trees greater than 14"dbh.
Bur Oak	Generally free of defects	Resistant to decay. Highly adapted to load (wind).
Cottonwood	Decay, Branch breakage	Branch breakage: risk increases in trees greater than 16"dbh.
Elms	Dead wood	Dutch elm disease. Tolerant to disturbance.

Common Defects of Eastern Hardwoods

Species	Common Defects	Comments & Causes
Hackberry	Weak unions, Decay, Branch breakage	Branch breakage: risk increases in trees greater than 16"dbh.
Honey locust	Canker	Thyronectria canker disease.
Northern Red Oak	Branch breakage, Decay	Brown rots, extensive decay with few signs or symptoms. Canker rot, disease. Branch breakage: risk increases in trees greater than 16"dbh.
Norway Maple	Weak unions, Cracks, Cankers, Decay, Deadwood	Multiple weak unions, cracks, cankers, and decay. Not acclimated to conditions found in the mid-west.
Other Red Oaks	Weak unions, Branch breakage, Decay, Deadwood	Sensitive to stress, dieback, and decay.
Silver Maple	Weak unions, Cracks, Cankers, Decay, Dead wood	Common to find multiple weak branch unions and decay in branches in mature trees. Species becomes too large for use in urban areas. High incidence of branch failures during storm events. Branch breakage: risk increases in trees greater than 16"dbh.
Sugar Maple	Dead wood, Weak unions, Cankers, Decay	Weak unions are common, opposite bud set. Eutypella canker disease, (cobra head). Maple decline is common in urban areas.
Willow	Branch breakage, Decay	Little resistance to decay. Branch breakage: risk increases in trees greater than 14"dbh.

Common Defects of Conifers

CONIFERS

Species	Common Defects	Comments & Causes
Larch	Decay, Windthrow	Shallow root systems.
Red Pine	Dead wood, Decay	Windthrow, Bark beetles, Canker rot.
Spruces	Windthrow	Spruce have shallow root systems. Windthrow increases in trees greater than 14"dbh.
Tamarack	Windthrow	Shallow root systems.
White Pine	Dead wood, Branch breakage Cankers	High risk of branch breakage during storm events. Dead tops, white pine blister rust disease.

List is not exhaustive. Failures for reasons other than those listed can be expected.

Terminology and Other Useful Information

Risk Assessment
The process of evaluating the potential of a tree to fail, the environment that may contribute to tree failure, and a potential target.

Target
Targets include facilities, people, and personal property. Targets may be prioritized by intensity of use.

Trees With High Risk of Failure
Trees with these defects and full crowns are failing, have failed, or have a high risk of failing soon. Corrective action must be taken as soon as possible.

Trees With Lower Risk of Failure
Immediate corrective action is currently not necessary. Included bark stem and branch unions will eventually fail.

Exposure and Risk of Failure
Risk of failure increases for the most exposed, and tallest trees. Quantifying actual load for individual trees may be possible (read Mattheck).

Leaning Trees
All trees lean to some extent. Determine if the lean is natural or if the tree is failing. Look for signs of failure. Increase caution when leaning trees are associated with past or recent construction damage, trenching or soil compaction, and when additional defects are found at the base of a leaning stem. Leaning trees can be the tough to evaluate and the hard to defend.

Branch Breakage
Refers to branches that fail in generally mature and over-mature trees. As decay moves from the stem into the base of large untapered branches on decurrent stem forms, branch failures increase. Species well adapted to load (wind) produce large tapered branches.

Open and Closed Cracks
Weak points are counter balanced by natural growth stresses. Pressure in the circumference around the stem during the growing season closes the crack. Absent during the dormant season the cracks on temperate climate species will open. The same principle may play a role in summer branch drop. During dry periods cracks may form on large untapered branches.

Poor Tree Architecture
Watch for unbalanced crowns and branches, branches with sharp twists, and harp branches.

Tree Species, Age, Size, and Condition
All play a role in the type, extent, and severity of defects. Defects in trees in poor condition will increase in severity over time. Trees in good condition with lower risk defects have an opportunity to repair over time.

Decay
Wounds start the process that leads to decay in trees. Avoid wounds, prune properly.

Crown Reduction Thinning
Thinning the crown, reducing the size and weight can reduce the risk of failure.

Signs and Symptoms of Decay

On stems and branches; holes, wounds cavities, cracks, fruiting structures, dead wood, dead and loose bark, stem bulge, swellings, and ribs. Squirrels are not external indicators of internal decay. Around the root collar; look for grade changes, soil mounding, and no root flares, or less prominent root flares.

Computing Ratio (remaining wall)

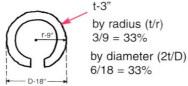

t-3"
by radius (t/r)
3/9 = 33%
by diameter (2t/D)
6/18 = 33%

Root Protection Zone

When possible use one foot for each inch of stem diameter (dbh) as radius.

Estimating Tree Fall Distance

Use total height plus 10%. If the tree has an exceptionally large root plate increase to total height plus 15%.

Inspections

Inspect once a year and following storm events. Inspections are best done during the leaf off season for temperate climate species. Be systematic and complete.

Documentation

Always document your evaluations and actions. Use a standard form that records species, defects, recommendations, and actions taken.

Treatment Options

Mitigation can range from increasing the awareness of the risk to specific actions. Actions include continued monitoring, moving the target, rerouting the traffic, pruning the tree, reducing the crown weight, fencing or closing the area, or

Safety Issues for Arborists

Accidents are caused by falls, falling branches and trees, and electrocution. Do a complete and systematic inspection before felling, climbing, rigging, or cabling.

Falls...fatalities increase for falls above 15 meters. Above 15 meters is an increased danger zone. ***Electrical hazards***...fatalities increase for blind indirect contacts. In aerial lifts, watch your back. ***Rigging***...the shock loading of large tree parts that swing can cause the stem below to fail. When rigging either to remove the entire tree or large limbs inspect for structural integrity of the root plate and main stem. Check leaning trees for advanced decay in the roots, or severed root systems.

Decay...as the ratio of sound wood in the outer wall decreases to near 20% or less the tree may not be safe to climb. The ratio may need to be greater than 35% or more if the tree is to be used for rigging. Consider using cranes or other rigging options for trees with low ratios and weak cross-sections. Use false crotches and blocks to avoid stress and injury to the tree.
Leaning trees...as the load changes the tree can spring back.
Cracks...consider the location and extent of compromise.

When climbing do not tie into or rely on branches that are cracked, decayed or dead. Keep feet, hands, and ropes out of tight V-shaped crotches.

Storm damaged trees

The greatest risk is unexpected movement! Be aware that everything has changed mechanically! Under normal conditions branches are loaded above by tension, and below by compression. Once lodged or on the ground the forces are opposite. The top is under compression and the bottom is under tension. Proceed with caution. Lighten first, work from the outside in, then from the top down. ***Lightning Struck Trees***...Use caution, unknown structural integrity is the issue.

Sources: Personal communications with John Ball of South Dakota, and Tom Dunlap of Minnesota, and ANSI Z133.1, American National Standards for Tree Care Operations.